Look,
Find &
Learn

U.S. History

Illustrator: Gary Ciccarelli

Writer: Linda Williams Aber

Consultant: Darrell J. Kozlowski

Louis Weber, CEO
Publications International, Ltd.
7373 North Cicero Avenue
Lincolnwood, Illinois 60712

Permission is never granted for commercial purposes.

Manufactured in USA.

8 7 6 5 4 3 2 1

ISBN: 1-4127-1047-2

Publications International, Ltd.

Contents

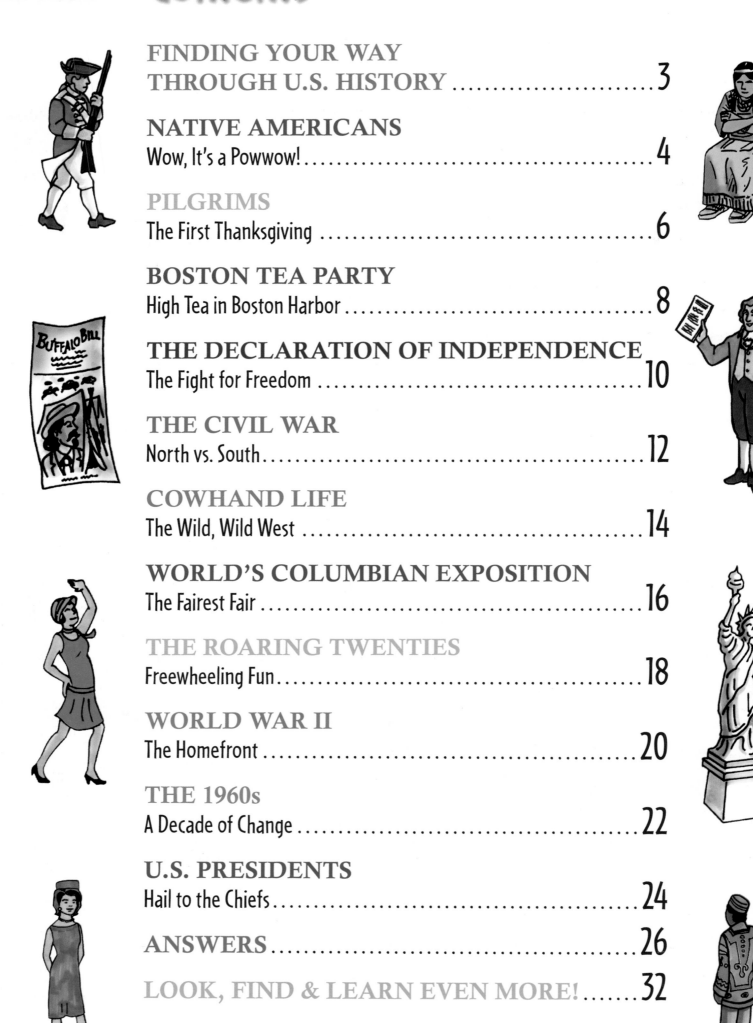

Finding Your Way Through U.S. History

LOOK at amazing illustrations of key periods of U.S. history…FIND all kinds of things hidden in each picture…and LEARN tons of cool facts about historic events—all in one awesome book! *Look, Find & Learn: U.S. History* gives the lowdown on some of the most significant people, places, and dates in American history.

Each illustration is bursting with hidden items for you to discover. Some will be easy to spot, while others will require more effort—and maybe even a magnifying glass! Surrounding each colorful scene are smaller pictures with fascinating facts and amazing information about the time period, making each search a fun learning experience. The facts will make the most sense if you start in the top left corner and continue reading counterclockwise.

In some cases we've altered history just a bit so we could pack in as much information as possible—and add even more fun for you! For example, in the illustration about U.S. presidents, you'll find George Washington, George W. Bush, and every president in between all in the same place!

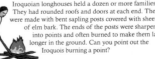

Often you'll be asked to find more than one of the same thing. Keep in mind that even items that are only partly shown should be counted. If you're completely stumped, turn to pages 26–31 for the answers. When you've found everything and want more, turn to page 32 for more challenges!

So start looking, finding, and learning—the fun will never end!

NATIVE AMERICANS — Wow, It's a Powwow!

When Christopher Columbus came to America, he thought he had landed in India, so he called everyone he met "Indians." But these people were actually Native Americans who had lived on this land for thousands of years. They taught European settlers about the land, its many natural resources, and much more!

Instead of money, Native Americans used small beads made from shells. They called these beads wampum. The tribes especially valued beads made from the dark purple, black, and white quahog clamshells. Don't clam up now—find the three strings of wampum.

Native American children ran races and held wrestling contests and archery matches. They played Chunkey, which was like bowling with a stone disc, and players threw sticks at a rolling hoop in a game called Hoop and Pole. Girls made Cat's Cradles with string and played with cornhusk dolls. Can you find the real cat near the Cat's Cradle?

Clothes were typically made from deerskin. Treated animal hides were used for shirts, leggings, dresses, skirts, and moccasins. To decorate clothing, Native Americans used feathers, shells, stones, paint, and porcupine-quill embroidery. Put your finger on the five feathers in this scene that might be used to decorate a new deerskin shirt.

In the 1500s, when Europeans first sailed to America, there were two great tribes of Native Americans in the Eastern Woodlands. They were the Algonquian-speaking people and the Iroquoian-speaking people. Search high and low for the members of each tribe saying hi to one other.

Native Americans were hunter-gatherers. The women gathered berries and nuts in the woods. The men hunted for animals, or game, with their bows and arrows. Sometimes they even disguised themselves as animals. Hunt down the hunter "hiding" in a hide.

Northeast tribes used canoes for transportation. They made a framework of spruce wood and covered it with pieces of birch bark. Can you find this chest made of birch bark?

Algonquian wigwams were shaped like cones and made of pole frames covered with birch bark or animal hides. They were built over a shallow pit with dirt piled around the base. Fires in the center provided heat and light. Hop to it and find the animal that's all fired up.

The Algonquians and Iroquois fished the rivers, streams, lakes, and ponds. They caught fish with harpoons, hooks, nets, and traps. Do you think you can catch the ten fish in this scene?

The Iroquois were good farmers. They called their three most important crops—maize, beans, and squash—the Three Sisters and planted them together on small hills. Can you pick out two squash that have already been picked?

The Algonquians were a patriarchal society, which meant men led the community. The Iroquois were a matriarchal society, led by women. A clan mother who owned the crops and shared homes headed each clan. Find the clan mother in this Iroquoian village.

Some Native Americans lived in permanent villages. They made clearings in the woods near streams or rivers and surrounded their villages with tall walls made from sharpened logs stuck in the ground. Other tribes were nomads and changed village sites depending on where they could find food. Get moving and spot the family that's moving out.

Iroquoian longhouses held a dozen or more families. They had rounded roofs and doors at each end. They were made with bent sapling posts covered with sheets of elm bark. The ends of the posts were sharpened into points and often burned to make them last longer in the ground. Can you point out the Iroquois burning a point?

You'll have tons of fun searching for the items in each scene. Remember to start in the top left corner and read counterclockwise.

Wow, It's a Powwow!

When Christopher Columbus came to America, he thought he had landed in India, so he called everyone he met "Indians." But these people were actually Native Americans who had lived on this land for thousands of years. They taught European settlers about the land, its many natural resources, and much more!

In the 1500s, when Europeans first sailed to America, there were two great tribes of Native Americans in the Eastern Woodlands. They were the Algonquian-speaking people and the Iroquoian-speaking people. Search high and low for the members of each tribe saying hi to one other.

Native Americans were hunter-gatherers. The women gathered berries and nuts in the woods. The men hunted for animals, or game, with their bows and arrows. Sometimes they even disguised themselves as animals. Hunt down the hunter "hiding" in a hide.

The Algonquians and Iroquois fished the rivers, streams, lakes, and ponds. They caught fish with harpoons, hooks, nets, and traps. Do you think you can catch the ten fish in this scene?

The Iroquois were good farmers. They called their three most important crops—maize, beans, and squash—the Three Sisters and planted them together on small hills. Can you pick out two squash that have already been picked?

The Algonquians were a patriarchal society, which meant men led the community. The Iroquois were a matriarchal society, led by women. A clan mother who owned the crops and shared homes headed each clan. Find the clan mother in this Iroquoian village.

Instead of money, Native Americans used small beads made from shells. They called these beads wampum. The tribes especially valued beads made from the dark purple, black, and white quahog clamshells. Don't clam up now—find the three strings of wampum.

Native American children ran races and held wrestling contests and archery matches. They played Chunkey, which was like bowling with a stone disc, and players threw sticks at a rolling hoop in a game called Hoop and Pole. Girls made Cat's Cradles with string and played with cornhusk dolls. Can you find the real cat near the Cat's Cradle?

Clothes were typically made from deerskin. Treated animal hides were used for shirts, leggings, dresses, skirts, and moccasins. To decorate clothing, Native Americans used feathers, shells, stones, paint, and porcupine-quill embroidery. Put your finger on the five feathers in this scene that might be used to decorate a new deerskin shirt.

Northeast tribes used canoes for transportation. They made a framework of spruce wood and covered it with pieces of birch bark. Can you find this chest made of birch bark?

Algonquian wigwams were shaped like cones and made of pole frames covered with birch bark or animal hides. They were built over a shallow pit with dirt piled around the base. Fires in the center provided heat and light. Hop to it and find the animal that's all fired up.

Some Native Americans lived in permanent villages. They made clearings in the woods near streams or rivers and surrounded their villages with tall walls made from sharpened logs stuck in the ground. Other tribes were nomads and changed village sites depending on where they could find food. Get moving and spot the family that's moving out.

Iroquoian longhouses held a dozen or more families. They had rounded roofs and doors at each end. They were made with bent sapling posts covered with sheets of elm bark. The ends of the posts were sharpened into points and often burned to make them last longer in the ground. Can you point out the Iroquois burning a point?

The First Thanksgiving

When people talk of Thanksgiving, they usually talk turkey. Although it may be the main course for most people today, turkey was just one of many dishes at the very first Thanksgiving. The Pilgrims and their neighbors from the Wampanoag tribe ate fish, geese, and lots of vegetables from the year's plentiful harvest.

On September 16, 1620, the *Mayflower* set sail from Plymouth, England, to America. Some of the more than 100 passengers were Separatists—a religious group that wanted to separate themselves from the Church of England. Another group, called Strangers, were farmers and tradespeople looking for a better life. It looks like one of the Separatists got separated from her Bible. Can you find it?

For 66 days the *Mayflower* sailed across the stormy Atlantic Ocean. The long trip and close quarters led to disagreements between the Separatists and Strangers. Once the ship docked, the two groups signed the Mayflower Compact to resolve their differences and to make sure both groups had equal say in all decisions. They joined together and called themselves Pilgrims. Pin down the pen that perhaps was picked to sign the Mayflower Compact.

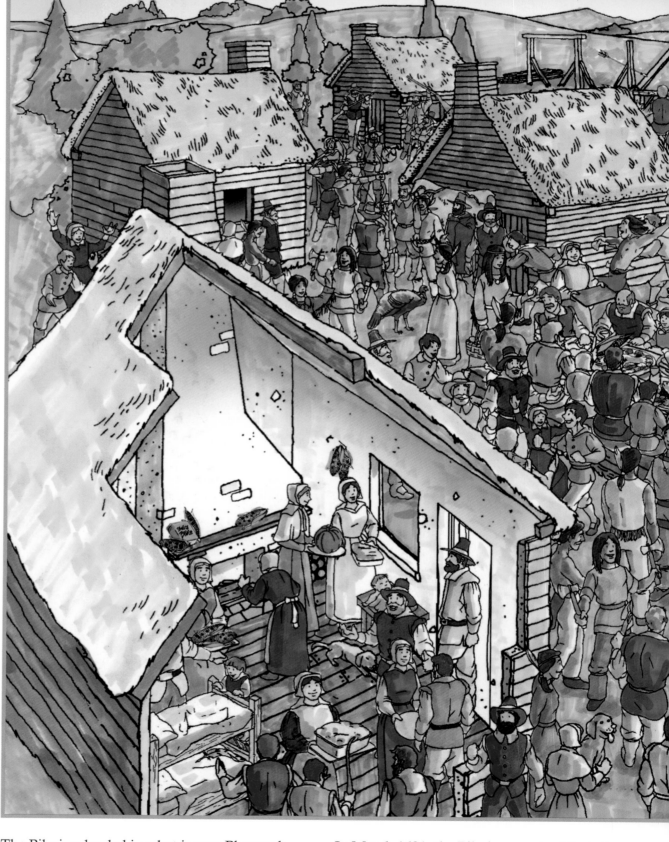

The Pilgrims landed in what is now Plymouth, Massachusetts. Faced with a cold winter, the Pilgrims quickly built a common house for everyone to sleep in. The house didn't have much more room or privacy than the *Mayflower!* Shh … quietly find the two crying babies who can't fall asleep.

In March 1621, the Pilgrims received their first visitor, a Native American from the Wampanoag tribe. The Pilgrims were frightened until he said, "Welcome. I am Samoset!" He brought a deer hide as a gift to welcome the Pilgrims to the neighborhood. Do you see where the hide is hiding?

Before the meal, the Pilgrims offered prayers of thanksgiving for their plentiful crops. Then they feasted on deer meat, cornbread, pumpkins, fish, geese, turkey, and more. Can you spot the Pilgrim who is as stuffed as a turkey?

During the three-day celebration, the Pilgrims and Wampanoags played games, ran races, and beat drums. The Native Americans showed off their skills with a bow and arrow, and the Pilgrims demonstrated how to use a musket. Point out nine arrows.

Thanks in part to Squanto's helpful hints, the harvest of 1621 was very successful. The Pilgrims had plenty of food to put away for the winter. To celebrate their good fortune, they invited the Wampanoags to a feast. About 90 Native Americans came to the party, including their leader. Feast your eyes on the Wampanoag's chief.

Squanto also taught the Pilgrims all kinds of tips for survival: how to tap maple trees for their sweet sap, how to plant Indian corn, and how to put a dead herring (a fish) on top of the seeds to fertilize the corn and make it grow quickly. Put your eye on 11 ears of corn.

On his next visit, Samoset brought along Squanto, a Native American who had been kidnapped by English fishermen and sold as a slave in Spain. Squanto had escaped to England, but he later returned to America and joined the Wampanoags. Squint to find Squanto in this scene.

A skilled hunter, Squanto helped the Pilgrims shoot deer and wild turkey roaming the woods. Then he taught them how to tan animal hides for clothing. Gobble up the three wild turkeys in this scene.

High Tea in Boston Harbor

In the late 1700s, after years of war, England needed money. King George III had a TEA-riffic idea: Tax everything England sent to the American colonies, including tea! But the colonists protested, wanting a say in their own government: "No taxation without representation!" they cried, and refused to pay the taxes. And that was just the beginning of what became the most famous tea party in history!

Keeping the American colonies afloat was bankrupting England. First, King George III passed the Stamp Act of 1765, which placed a tax on all printed materials, including newspapers, books, and playing cards. Then came the Townshend Acts. England used these taxes to pay British officials' salaries. Do you see where one colonist put five of his favorite books to avoid the tax?

These taxes made the colonists so angry that some of them formed a protest group called the Sons of Liberty. You are at liberty to spot Samuel Adams, the leader of the Sons of Liberty.

Not only did the colonists not want to pay taxes, but they also wanted a vote and a voice in British Parliament. Their slogan was "No taxation without representation." One member of Parliament isn't sitting pretty here—he's lost his wig! Can you spot it?

Many of the colonists boycotted, or stopped, drinking tea as a protest against the Tea Act. This almost forced England's East India Company out of business, so the king made it the only company allowed to sell tea in the colonies. In your thirst for knowledge, find three other beverages the colonists might have drunk during the tea boycott.

Although the Sons of Liberty were surrounded by British warships in the harbor, no attempt was made to arrest those involved in the raid. But later, England shut down Boston Harbor and took away the colonists' right to rule themselves. These Intolerable Acts sparked the American Revolution. Feel free to find the British soldier, or Redcoat, ready to defend England.

Not all of the tea chests sank, so other colonists rowed into the harbor to break open the floating chests with their oars and spill the tea into the harbor. Set your sights on the colonist who "spilled" into the harbor himself.

Armed with tomahawks, the Sons of Liberty swarmed the decks, opened the hatches, and took out 342 chests of tea. They split them open with their tomahawks and dumped the tea into the harbor. Four tomahawks were dropped. Take a swing at finding them.

In the dead of night on December 16, about 50 members of the Sons of Liberty went to the local blacksmith shop, put coal dust on their faces, and disguised themselves as Native Americans. They went to the harbor where the three ships were anchored. Oops! One of the Sons of Liberty forgot to change out of his night shirt. Do you see him?

UNLOAD TEA BY DECEMBER 17... OR ELSE! SIGNED, *Governor Hutchinson*

Many colonial tea wholesalers refused to allow the East India Company's ships to enter their harbors. But the royal governor of Massachusetts, Thomas Hutchinson, had relatives and friends in the tea business, so he let the *Eleanor,* the *Beaver,* and the *Dartmouth* dock in Boston. Look high and low for Governor Hutchinson at high tea with his friends.

The Boston dockworkers refused to unload the tea. Governor Hutchinson warned them that if they didn't unload it by December 17, 1773, his warships in the harbor would seize the tea and charge the colonists taxes on it anyway. Sit up and take notice of his threatening notice.

9

The Fight for Freedom

After the Boston Tea Party, England's King George III was angrier than ever. He passed a series of laws that became known as the Intolerable Acts. For the colonists, this was the last straw. They decided to create the Declaration of Independence. Feel free to learn more about the events that led to the signing of that document.

Paul Revere was an express rider who carried news and messages for the Boston Committee of Correspondence. On the evening of April 18, 1775, he warned two patriots, John Hancock and Samuel Adams, that the British were coming to arrest them. Look far and wide for Paul Revere on his famous ride.

Revere hung two lanterns in the bell tower of Christ Church in Boston to signal that the Redcoats, as the British soldiers were known, were coming "by sea" across the Charles River rather than "by land." Help Paul Revere find two lanterns that match this one so he can hang them in the bell tower.

When 700 Red-coats arrived in Lexington, Massachusetts, the morning of April 19, they were met by 77 Minutemen—farmers and laborers trained to be ready to fight "in a minute." When a Minuteman accidentally fired his musket, it became known as "the shot heard 'round the world" because it began the American Revolution. Look 'round to find the famous musket.

On May 10, 1775, the Second Continental Congress met in Philadelphia. The Congress elected as its president wealthy Bostonian John Hancock. On June 15, they voted to appoint George Washington general and commander-in-chief of the new Continental Army. In this scene, General Washington is ready for battle, except for one important part of his military outfit. Hats off to you if you can find his hat.

On July 4, 1776, the Declaration of Independence was read aloud for the first time at Independence Hall in Philadelphia. During the celebration, the first American flag flew, heralding the birth of a new nation. Celebrate the Fourth of July by finding six of Betsy Ross's new flags.

On June 7, 1776, Richard Henry Lee, a Virginia delegate to the Continental Congress, presented a formal resolution calling for America to declare its independence from Britain. The youngest member of the Continental Congress, Thomas Jefferson, was chosen to prepare the first draft of the declaration, which he completed in only one day! Can you find him writing the Declaration of Independence?

Up until that time, the colonies and militias used many different flags. Some are famous, such as the Rattlesnake Flag used by the Continental Navy, with its slogan, "Don't Tread on Me." Don't get rattled by the snake: Find the Navy's flag.

In May, the Congressional Committee called on Betsy Ross, a young widow who ran an upholstery business, to make a flag that would be different from the British Union Jack. They said, "The flag of the United States shall be thirteen stripes, alternate red and white; that the union be thirteen stars, white in a blue field, representing a new constellation." You'll be a star if you can find Betsy Ross.

The first major conflict between British and American troops occurred in Boston at the Battle of Bunker Hill. The Americans were not to fire until they saw "the whites of their eyes." There are lots of Redcoats in this scene, but can you also find a red coat that looks like this?

In Philadelphia on January 9, 1776, Thomas Paine, a well-respected writer and editor, published a 50-page pamphlet called *Common Sense.* The booklet criticized King George III and argued for American independence. It became an instant bestseller. With a little common sense, you may find the pamphlet.

NORTH vs. SOUTH

Did you know there was a time when the United States wasn't united? During the 19th century, the South used slaves to work the cotton plantations, but the North was largely opposed to slavery. This led to a war between the North and the South from 1861 to 1865 that pitted neighbor against neighbor, brother against brother.

By the 1800s, the South's economy was heavily dependent on cotton. Southern plantation owners used African slaves to work their fields. Around this time, Eli Whitney invented the cotton gin, a machine that could remove the seeds from cotton bolls more quickly than human hands. The invention made slave labor even more important. Pick out the cotton gin in this scene.

Factories in the North had modern equipment that made clothing and home supplies. Many Northerners didn't approve of slavery, in part because the cheap labor created competition for their factories. Others, called abolitionists, wanted to end slavery altogether. Can you find the famous abolitionist Harriet Tubman, who rescued close to 300 slaves?

Abraham Lincoln, elected president in 1860, was opposed to slavery and wanted the United States to remain one nation. This angered the South, causing 11 states to leave the Union and form the Confederacy, where slavery would remain legal. The Confederacy elected Jefferson Davis as its president. Flag down the Confederate flag in three places.

On April 12, 1861, the Confederates fired on Fort Sumter, a Union fort in South Carolina. The Northern soldiers inside the fort returned fire. The battle lasted two days before the fort surrendered. The Civil War had begun. Don't give up—find the white flag of surrender.

Gettysburg was the bloodiest conflict ever to take place on American soil. About 23,000 Union soldiers died; the South lost around 28,000. Homes and churches throughout Gettysburg were turned into hospitals to care for the wounded. During the Civil War, Clara Barton established an organization to provide supplies to wounded soldiers, which later became the American Red Cross. Can you come across Clara Barton?

On the second day of the Battle of Gettysburg, General Lee, with help from General George E. Pickett, sent more than 10,000 Confederates across an open field in what was called Pickett's Charge. But the Union soldiers were on three sides and opened fire, killing thousands of Confederate troops. Pick out Pickett leading his troops.

Hoping to find shoes and other supplies for his soldiers, Confederate General Robert E. Lee ordered the invasion of Gettysburg, Pennsylvania, in July 1863. Although his army initially pushed back the Union Army, more troops arrived. Take a step toward finding three Confederate soldiers in need of shoes.

On January 1, 1863, President Lincoln issued the Emancipation Proclamation. This document stated "that all persons held as slaves" within the rebellious states "are, and henceforward shall be, free." It also allowed African-American men to join the Union Army and Navy. Almost 200,000 African-American soldiers and sailors fought for the Union and freedom. Feel free to find this man with his new uniform.

Some young people in the South joined the Confederate Army to save their families' plantations. Many Northern boys followed their fathers into the Union Army to fight against slavery. In some states, a family might have had one son fighting for the Confederates while another son defended the Union Army. Join these two brothers going their separate ways.

The Wild, Wild West

Do you think of the American cowboy as a gun-totin', hard-ridin', fast-shootin' hero who fights off rustlers and brings bad guys to justice? That's partly true. But they were also lonely, dirty danger-seekers with few friends other than their horse. Do you think you'd like to live this life?

The first cowboys, called *vaqueros,* were from Spain. The American cowboy inherited the title, equipment, roping techniques, and vocabulary—lariat, rodeo, buckaroo—from the vaqueros. Lasso a vaquero wearing this hat as he shows an American cowboy some roping techniques.

After the Civil War, many former soldiers and slaves rushed to the West to seek their fortunes as cowboys. Ranchers hired them to round up stray longhorns, brand them, and drive them north to market. Can you put your finger on these five brands?

The pay at the end of a cattle drive—which usually lasted three months—was about $100. Dodge City, Kansas, was one of the most popular trail towns in America. There, at the end of a drive, a cowboy could get a bath, a haircut, and new clothes. The town was also known for its wild saloons and gambling. Tag the three cowboys who still have price tags on their new clothes.

Cowboys needed protection from head to toe—from ten-gallon Stetson hats and bandannas to flannel shirts and rawhide chaps. They wore boots with pointed toes to help them easily slip into horse stirrups and with two-inch heels to keep them from sliding out. Cowboys also carried a knife in their waistband and a revolver on their hip to shoot rattlesnakes. Find the three blue bandannas on cowboys in this scene.

A famous cowgirl in Buffalo Bill's Wild West Show was the markswoman Annie Oakley. Dubbed "Little Sure Shot" (she was five feet tall), she won many awards for her sharpshooting and dazzled audiences far and wide. Can you find Annie's medals?

In addition to races, sharpshooting contests, and rodeo-style events, the Wild West Show featured historical plays, such as *Battle of the Little Big Horn*. Native Americans were in many of the scenes, often shown attacking people while Buffalo Bill or one of his colleagues rode in to save the day. Spot nine Native Americans.

Buffalo Bill's show-business career began in Chicago, Illinois, when he was 26 years old. His Wild West Show was designed to both educate and entertain. He used a cast of hundreds as well as live buffalo, elk, cattle, and other animals. Do you see Buffalo Bill hanging this show flyer?

The coming of the railroads put many cowboys out of business. One cowboy who survived, William Cody, worked all kinds of jobs, including fur trapping, gold mining, and riding for the Pony Express. He later earned the nickname Buffalo Bill because of his skills as a buffalo hunter. Can you find the Pony Express pouch Buffalo Bill left behind?

Cowboys on the trail were often hungry. In 1866, a rancher named Charlie Goodnight fixed up an old army supply wagon with a food box in the back. The wagon carried a cook and food on trail rides. They named the wagon "chuck" after its inventor. Do you see the chuck wagon's coffeepot?

Trail drives were typically 700 to 1,200 miles long. The biggest danger, other than an attack by Native Americans, was a cattle stampede. If frightened, the cattle could harm anyone in their way. If they lost weight running, it lessened their value. Shoot! Can you find what frightened the cattle into a stampede?

The Fairest Fair

To celebrate the 400th anniversary of Christopher Columbus's voyage to America, a number of U.S. cities competed to hold the World's Columbian Exposition, or World's Fair, in 1892 and 1893. Chicago, Illinois, bid $10 million and won! The city turned 633 acres of Jackson Park on the shores of Lake Michigan into one of the greatest events in history of its kind. Let's go to the fair!

To get to the Exposition, visitors could take a train or a steamship from downtown Chicago to the South Pier. Then, for five cents, they could ride the world's first movable sidewalks to the Peristyle—the arch at the entrance to the Court of Honor on the Grand Basin. Admission to the fair was 50 cents. Can you sense something else at the Exposition that cost 50 cents?

Once visitors walked through the Peristyle, they found a city in shimmering white! Fairgoers called it the White City because 13 of the 14 main buildings were painted bright white. One building, the Transportation Building, didn't follow the rules—it had a multicolor look. Put your finger on the four sweet treats that are also multicolored.

The Manufactures and Liberal Arts Building housed exciting new products from America, Germany, Austria, China, Japan, France, Russia, and England, including colorful Tiffany stained glass, state-of-the-art Remington typewriters, all kinds of musical instruments, and the University of Chicago's 70-ton Yerkes telescope. Play around and find two guitars.

Inside the Transportation Building were wonderful displays of Pullman railroad cars and models of English warships. Try to find another, smaller vessel if it floats your boat.

 Many other famous "firsts" happened here. The post office introduced the first picture postcards and commemorative stamps. Many new products were introduced, including *Aunt Jemima* syrup, *Juicy Fruit* chewing gum, and *Cracker Jack* candied popcorn. And here's some food for thought: The hamburger was first introduced at the fair! Find seven people eating them up.

Some people were "uplifted" by the 6,000 art exhibits at the Palace of Fine Arts. Others were "lifted up" in the Captive Balloon on the Midway. Two trips were made every hour at $2 a journey. The balloon gave visitors a bird's-eye view of the exposition grounds at 1,500 feet. It's easy to spot the Captive Balloon . . . but do the five other balloons hidden in this scene pop out at you?

Urged by women's activist Susan B. Anthony and others, the fair committee decided that women should have a building of their own with special exhibits of their works. Artist Mary Cassatt's mural, "Modern Woman," showed freedom of expression in dance, while up on the Midway, the dancer Little Egypt expressed some freedom of her own. Make a move and find Little Egypt.

The fair committee created an entertainment area through the middle of the exposition called the Midway. The most popular ride was George Ferris's invention: You guessed it—the Ferris wheel! Plush revolving seats provided comfort to the passengers in each of the 36 cars. Each car could carry up to 60 passengers. Do you see George Ferris admiring his invention?

 The Electricity Building featured all the most modern electrical appliances: electric lamps, sewing machines, stoves, and more. Take a look at Thomas Edison's Tower of Light, with 18,000 light bulbs, and the world's first telegraph message. Reel in Edison's Kinetoscope (the first motion picture projector).

The Horticulture Building had eight greenhouses under a 180-foot dome, covering more than four acres of fairground space. Inside were a Japanese garden, 6,000 varieties of orchids, and a 35-foot tower of oranges. Pick out the five oranges that got away.

Freewheeling Fun

If someone called you "the cat's meow," would you take it as a compliment? You would if you had lived during the early 1920s. The slang of the era was "jive talk," which included such "hep" phrases as "the bee's knees" and "the pig's wings." Are you "jake"? You will be once you find out the facts about the wild days of flappers, talkies, and swing!

After World War I ended in 1918, America was ready for fun. Dancing was one way people let loose. Some of the popular dances at the time were the Charleston and the Black Bottom. Can you find this woman doing the Black Bottom?

Women earned many freedoms in the 1920s, including the right to vote. They also had more freedom in the clothes they wore—no more corsets!—and more time for fun outside the home. This new breed of young women were called flappers, an English word that described baby birds coming out of their nests with wildly flapping wings. Can you find a flapper at the voting booth?

Flappers "bobbed" their hair short and wore dresses that showed their legs—big no-nos according to the strict Victorian morals of the early 20th century. College boys wore raccoon coats and were called sheiks. Don't be a "flat tire"—find ten sheiks!

Radio broadcasting began in 1920, and the radio craze swept the nation after the first broadcast. Singers like Rudy Vallee and Jessica Dragonette were all the rage. Put your finger on two radios.

The Roaring Twenties were often called the Jazz Age. Louis "Satchmo" Armstrong, along with other African-American musicians, helped make jazz music popular. Satchmo wasn't a show-off, but he sure blew his own horn. Can you help him find his instrument?

Fads were the rage with the young people of the time. Wing-walking on small planes and flagpole-sitting were a couple of popular stunts. An ex-boxer named Alvin "Shipwreck" Kelly sat on a padded seat on top of a flagpole in Baltimore, Maryland, for 23 days and seven hours. Ouch! Can you spot him after his long sit-down?

Sports heroes during the Roaring Twenties included Yankee slugger Babe Ruth, who hit 60 home runs in one season. Red Grange, known as "The Galloping Ghost," scored 31 touchdowns for the University of Illinois. He helped make professional football popular when he played for the Chicago Bears. Can you find his jersey number in two places?

Did you know movies used to have no sound? In 1927, silent films got a voice when Al Jolson starred in a talkie called *The Jazz Singer.* Comedians Charlie Chaplin and Laurel and Hardy soon joined the trend and started making talking pictures, too. Can you find Charlie Chaplin? How about his trademark cane that he twirled as he walked?

On May 20, 1927, Charles Lindbergh, a young pilot, flew his single-engine plane from Long Island, New York, to Paris, France. The 3,610-mile nonstop flight took 33 hours and 29 minutes. "Lucky Lindy" became an instant hero. Can you find his aviator hat?

Henry Ford's "gas buggy" revolutionized the decade. It was called the Model T. By 1929, 23 million cars were on America's roads. Can you find the Ford logo?

This was the era of the Harlem Renaissance, when New York City's Harlem neighborhood became the home of African-American musicians. The flappers and their sheiks came to Harlem nightclubs like Cab Calloway's Cotton Club and The Savoy Ballroom. Instead of words, singers sang rhythmic syllables called scat. Can you find a cat that scat after hearing the nightclub singer?

THE HOMEFRONT

On December 7, 1941, Japanese planes bombed the American naval base at Pearl Harbor, Hawaii. Then Nazi Germany and its allies declared war on the United States. The American people united like never before. Thousands of Americans served in the armed forces overseas. At home, both men and women worked on farms, in mines, and in factories to help the war effort.

Throughout World War II, President Franklin D. Roosevelt guided America. With his generals, he planned the battles overseas. At home, he made sure the troops had enough guns, ammunition, planes, and tanks to win the war. The president even visited factories to meet the workers. Can you spot him?

More than 3.5 million women worked alongside 6 million men to make guns, ammunition, ships, planes, and tanks. American workers could turn out an entire cargo ship in 17 days! Look in the factory for this hard-working woman.

Because women worked outside the home, they no longer followed traditional roles and styles of dress. For safety reasons, working in a factory required women to wear pants—something few women had done before. Pants became a badge of honor. Women also wore a bandana, or snood, to hold back their hair. You should snoop around for the worker that forgot to put on her snood.

Rosie the Riveter was a fictional character used in advertising to encourage women to join the workforce. Many people believed that women were better at detail work because they were skilled at needlepoint. So, in addition to making weapons, women wired fuses on bombs and filled metal casings with gunpowder. Get to work and find the famous poster of Rosie.

The USO entertained troops all over the world. Comedians, singers, and dancers would fly to military bases to help cheer up the soldiers. Entertain yourself by finding the USO poster in this scene.

Almost every town had a Stage Door Canteen, where local women would serve refreshments to soldiers passing through town. There were always plenty of college students there to dance with the soldiers. Fish out the hat lost by one of the sailors.

To help the war effort, people were encouraged to plant a victory garden and grow carrots, peas, and tomatoes. Someone lost a garden spade … can you dig around for it?

Instead of receiving a bicycle or a toy train, many children received a war bond for their birthdays. Can you find two birthday presents hidden in this scene?

Many foods—meat, coffee, butter, cheese, sugar—were rationed, or equally divided, by a point system. There was also a limit on how often you could buy certain foods. For example, people could purchase only one pound of coffee every five weeks. Point out two things worth eight points.

All types of factories helped in the war effort. Factories that once made regular clothes made army uniforms. Instead of silk stockings, women wore leg makeup and painted a stocking seam up the back of their legs. There was even a tool designed to help make the line straight. Is your eye drawn to someone drawing a stocking seam?

During the war, Americans were given coupons and stamps that limited the amount of gas or food they could buy. Drivers received an "A" card that limited them to three gallons of gasoline a week. Spot someone who used up his three gallons of gas too soon!

A Decade of Change

The 1960s were packed with everything "new"—new music, new fashion, new rights, and new explorations. Many young people were rebelling against society, protesting the war, and promoting peace and love. Some minorities were working toward equal rights for all Americans, and the space program was sending people to the moon! Meanwhile, the music of the decade told about all of these life-changing events.

The 1960s started off with a dynamic new president: John F. Kennedy. He had many exciting ideas for the decade, including putting a man on the moon. Kennedy moved into the White House with his wife, Jacqueline, and their two children, Carolyn and John Jr. Let's play hide-and-seek: Find John Jr. hiding from his dad.

If you lived in the 1960s, you probably watched *The Ed Sullivan Show*—a television program that featured singers and other talented performers. Four rock singers from Liverpool, England—the Beatles—made their first U.S. television appearance on the show in 1964. The group's music was different from anything American kids had ever heard! Do you spy Ed Sullivan cheering on the Fab Four?

The Beatles became so popular that boys stopped cutting their hair to match the group's "mop tops." Other groovy fashion trends of the decade included clothes in psychedelic colors and "mod" miniskirts. Can you find eight people wearing this psychedelic shirt?

Along with new fashion trends, serious changes were taking place in society. Many people—both black and white—worked to gain equal rights for African-Americans. Dr. Martin Luther King, Jr., organized sit-ins and nonviolent protest marches. At the March on Washington, Dr. King gave his inspirational "I Have a Dream" speech. March on in and find the event's organizer, A. Philip Randolph.

On July 16, 1969, *Apollo 11* blasted off for the moon. While Mike Collins orbited the moon in the mother vehicle, *Columbia,* Neil Armstrong and "Buzz" Aldrin brought the lunar module *Eagle* down on the moon. Do you see Collins, Armstrong, and Aldrin? One of them has misplaced his space helmet…can you find it?

On May 5, 1961, Astronaut Alan B. Shepard, Jr., became the first American in space. He soared 116 miles above the earth aboard the space capsule *Freedom 7.* The word "freedom" appears two times in this scene. Feel free to find it.

The Haight Ashbury section of San Francisco, California, was the center of the hippie world in 1967. Hippies were young people who wanted the world to be a peaceful, loving place. What started in Haight Ashbury spread across the United States. Young people held peaceful sit-ins to protest the war, holding signs that said "Give Peace a Chance!" and "Flower Power!" Feel the power and find four Flower Children passing out flowers.

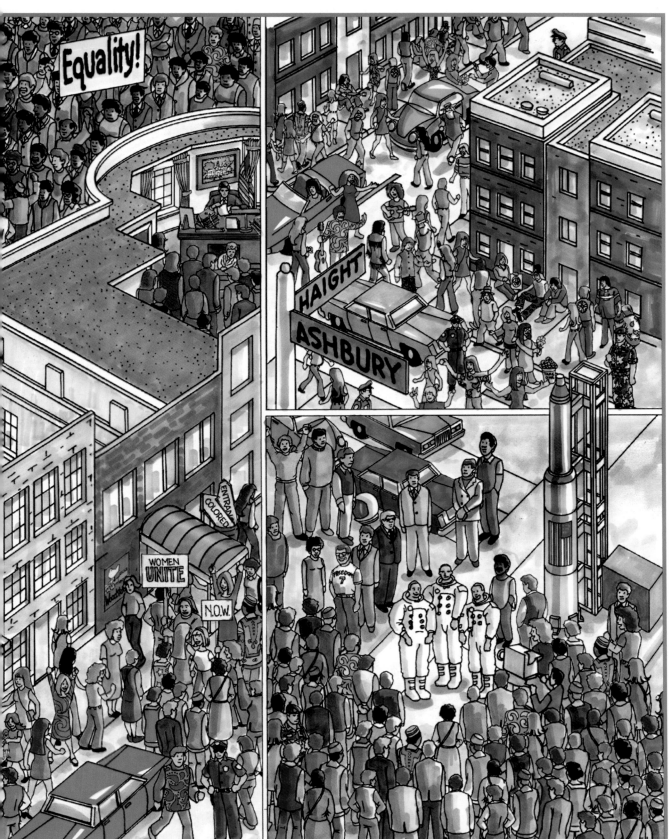

Fear of communism was very strong in this decade. Hearing that a small Asian country called South Vietnam was falling to the communists, America got involved, sending military advisers and troops. The Green Berets were an elite group of Marines that fought in Vietnam. Hats off to you if you find three Green Berets.

 Black Americans found ethnic identity in Africa's ancient kingdoms and arts and sciences. They began to wear African clothing, jewelry, and hairstyles and call themselves Afro-Americans. Where are the seven people wearing the African garment called a dashiki?

To help African-Americans and other minorities, President Lyndon Johnson encouraged Congress to pass the Civil Rights Act of 1964, which made it illegal for employers to discriminate because of race, creed, national origin, or sex. The new law also made segregation in such public places as hotels and restaurants illegal. Search for the segregation sign that went out with the trash.

23

Hail to the Chiefs!

Since George Washington became the first president in 1789, the United States has seen an amazing and unique group of leaders, including soldiers, lawyers, schoolteachers, farmers…even an actor! Each individual helped make the nation as powerful as it is today.

During the American Revolution, George Washington (1789–1797) led the colonial army to victory against the British. It was no surprise then when he was unanimously elected to be the first president. Washington helped develop what would become our nation's capital, Washington, D.C. He also chose the location for the White House, even though he never got to live there. Find the location of George Washington.

Thomas Jefferson (1801–1809) wanted to make the government smaller. But he doubled the size of the country in 1803 when he bought the land between the Mississippi River and the Rocky Mountains from Napoleon Bonaparte, the leader of France. Find Napoleon accepting Jefferson's offer of $15 million for the Louisiana Purchase.

When Abraham Lincoln (1861–1865) took office, the country was divided. Slavery was illegal in the northern states, while the southern states still depended on slave labor. Eleven southern states seceded from, or left, the United States, and the Civil War started soon after. The war ended when the South surrendered to the North in April 1865. A few days later, Lincoln was shot while watching the play *Our American Cousin* at Ford's Theatre in Washington, D.C. Search for the playbill from the play.

A former movie star and governor of California, Ronald Reagan (1981–1989) made people feel good about being American. He lowered taxes and raised defense spending, believing a strong United States was a safe United States. He played an important role in ending the Cold War. President Reagan loved jelly beans and kept a bowl of them on his desk. Bet you can't find the bowl of beans hidden in this scene.

President John F. Kennedy (1961–1963) brought hope to a nation facing the Cold War with the Soviet Union as well as tension from racial inequality at home. "Ask not what your country can do for you," he said. "Ask what you can do for your country." Sadly, Kennedy was assassinated after only 1,000 days as president. His wife, Jackie, was a popular and elegant first lady. Can you spot her?

"I Like Ike" was the campaign slogan for Dwight Eisenhower (1953–1961). And people really *did* like Ike! As Allied commander during World War II, he helped the nation win the war. He also introduced the Civil Rights Acts of 1957, which jump-started civil rights legislation. Would you like to find the "I Like Ike" poster?

When Franklin Delano Roosevelt (1933–1945) took office, the Great Depression had put millions out of work. He started the "New Deal," which featured job programs and bank reforms. FDR was the only president elected to four terms and was the first president to appear on TV. Tune in and find Roosevelt.

When President William McKinley was assassinated, 42-year-old Vice President Theodore (Teddy) Roosevelt (1901–1909) became the youngest president to take office. Did you know the teddy bear was named after him? According to one story, a couple who owned a toy store asked Roosevelt if they could call their bears "teddy bears." He said okay! Don't play around—find five teddy bears.

Woodrow Wilson (1913–1921) was president when World War I began. To help the Red Cross during the war, Wilson let sheep graze on the White House lawn. Their wool was sold to raise money for the war effort. Herd the one sheep that got away.

	tribe members		squash		Iroquois		birch bark item		cat
	hunter		clan mother		animal		feathers		wampum
	fish		family						

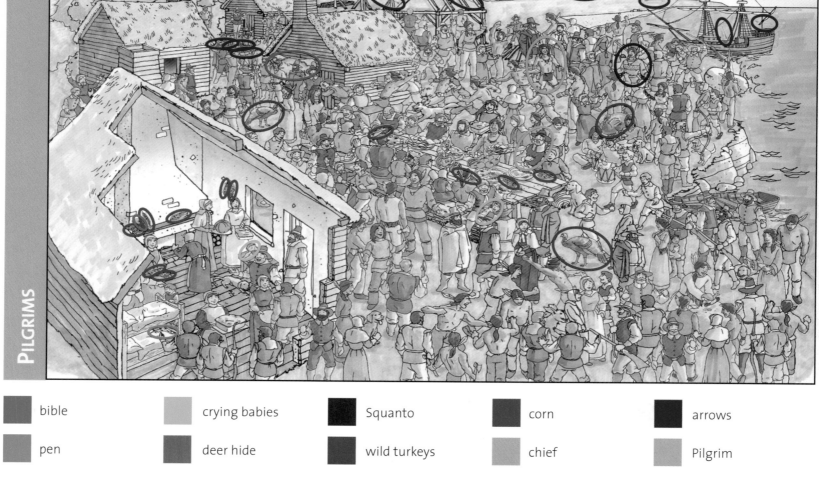

| | bible | | crying babies | | Squanto | | corn | | arrows |
| | pen | | deer hide | | wild turkeys | | chief | | Pilgrim |

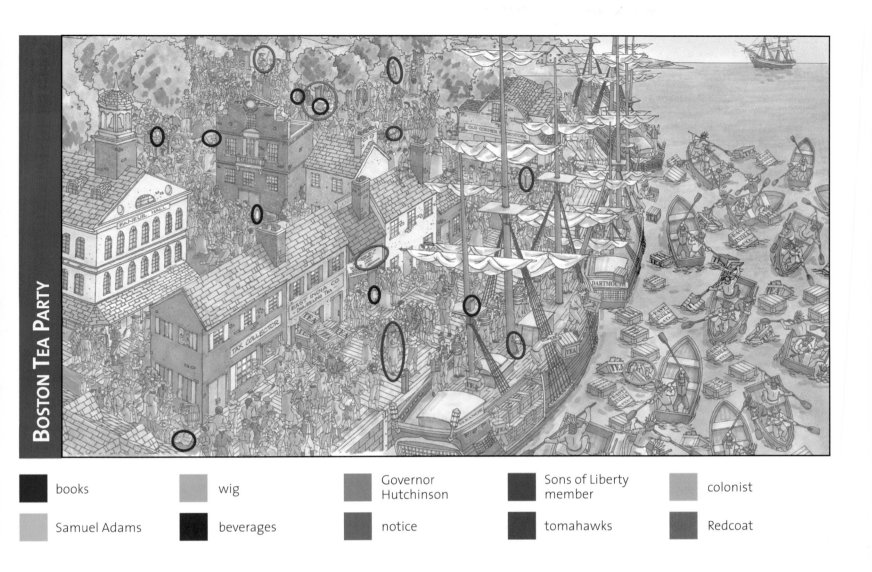

	books		wig		Governor Hutchinson		Sons of Liberty member		colonist
	Samuel Adams		beverages		notice		tomahawks		Redcoat

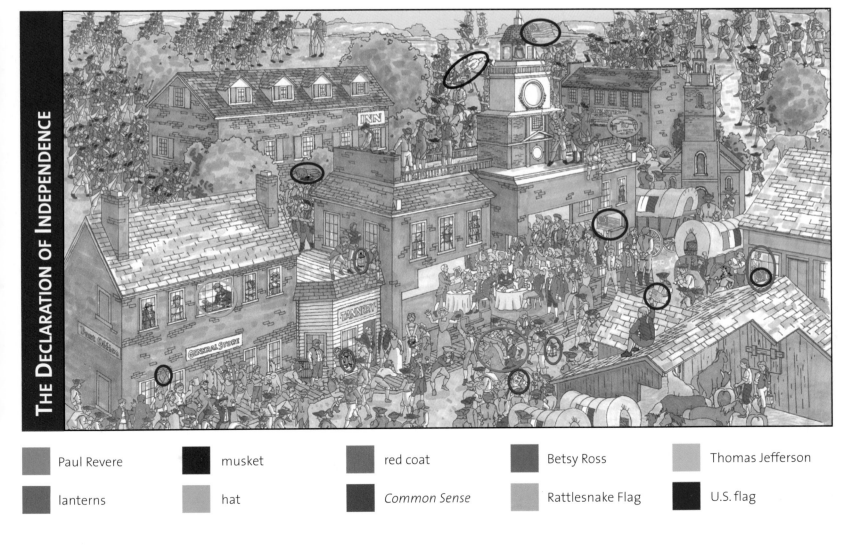

	Paul Revere		musket		red coat		Betsy Ross		Thomas Jefferson
	lanterns		hat		Common Sense		Rattlesnake Flag		U.S. flag

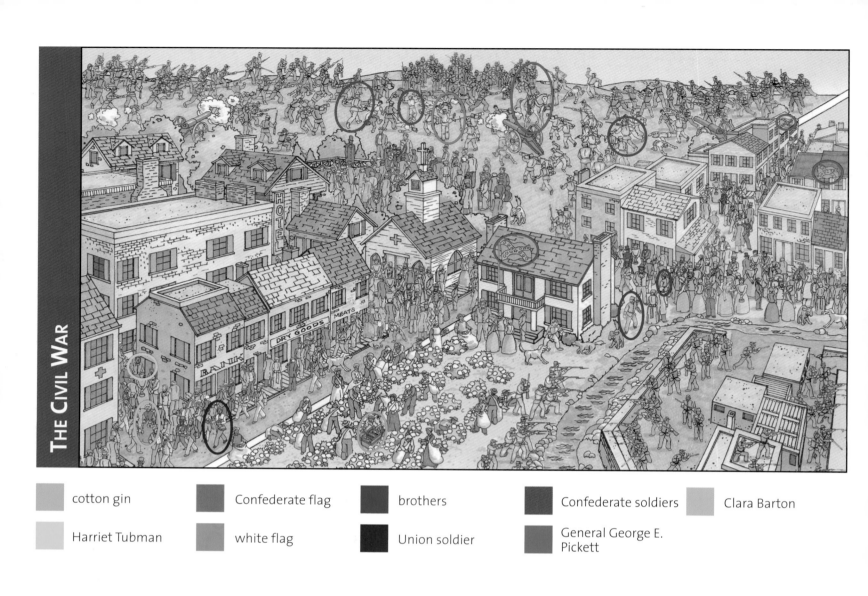

	cotton gin		Confederate flag		brothers		Confederate soldiers		Clara Barton
	Harriet Tubman		white flag		Union soldier		General George E. Pickett		

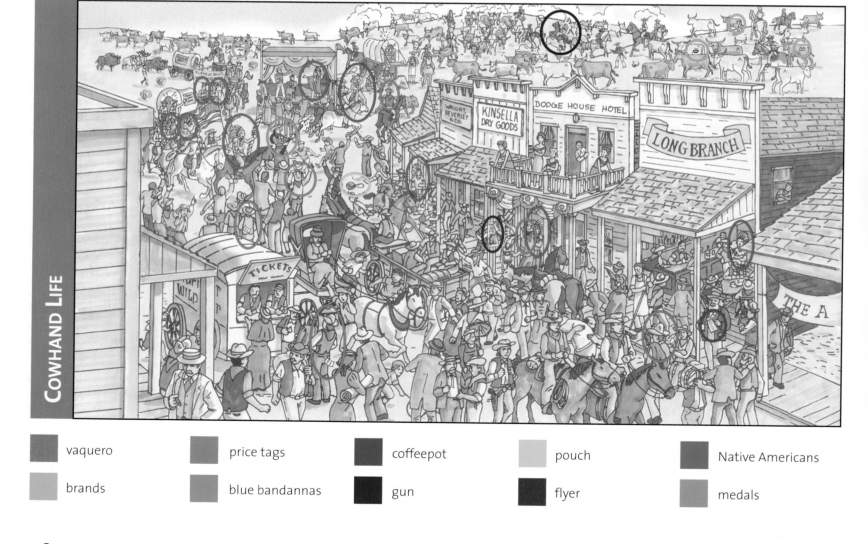

	vaquero		price tags		coffeepot		pouch		Native Americans
	brands		blue bandannas		gun		flyer		medals

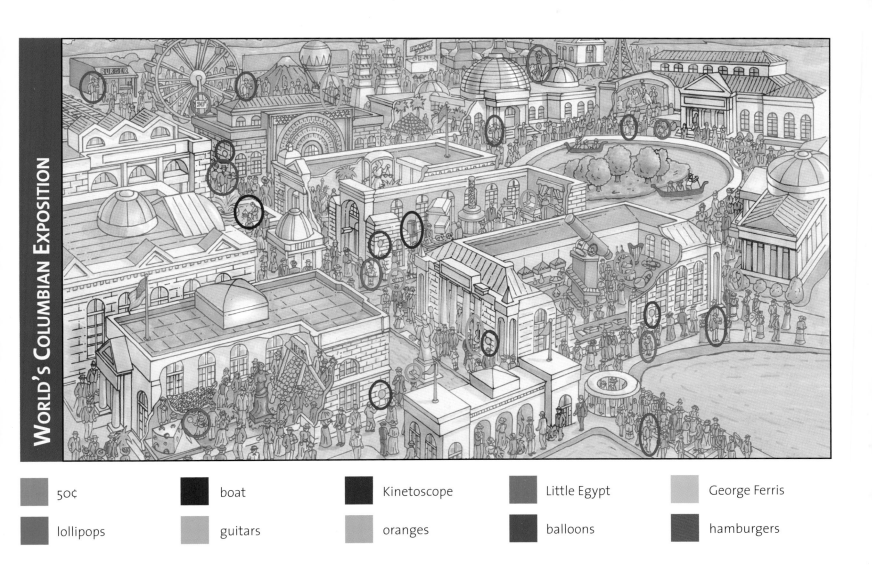

	50¢		boat		Kinetoscope		Little Egypt		George Ferris
	lollipops		guitars		oranges		balloons		hamburgers

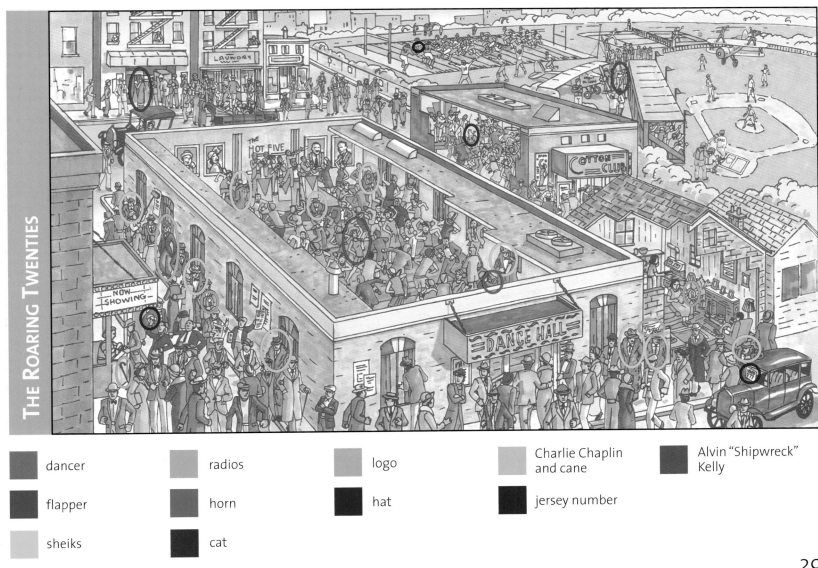

	dancer		radios		logo		Charlie Chaplin and cane		Alvin "Shipwreck" Kelly
	flapper		horn		hat		jersey number		
	sheiks		cat						

29

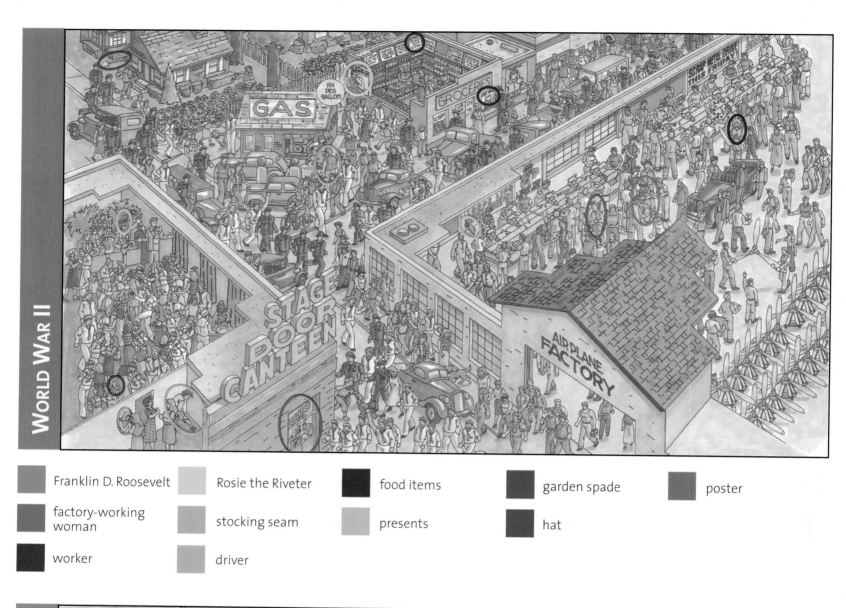

	Franklin D. Roosevelt		Rosie the Riveter		food items		garden spade		poster
	factory-working woman		stocking seam		presents		hat		
	worker		driver						

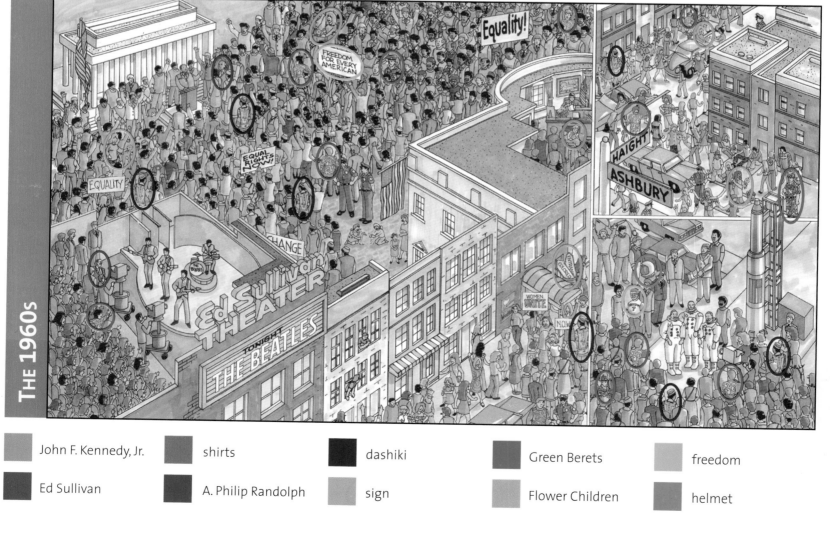

| | John F. Kennedy, Jr. | | shirts | | dashiki | | Green Berets | | freedom |
| | Ed Sullivan | | A. Philip Randolph | | sign | | Flower Children | | helmet |

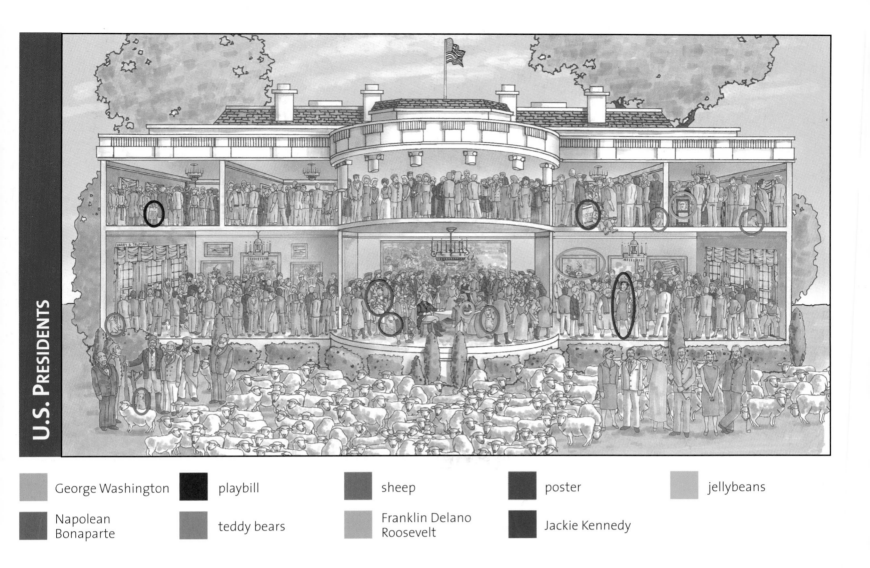

	George Washington		playbill		sheep		poster		jellybeans
	Napolean Bonaparte		teddy bears		Franklin Delano Roosevelt		Jackie Kennedy		

Look, Find & Learn Even More!

Think that's all there is? Not so fast! There are plenty more interesting items hidden within these pages. Are you up for the challenge? Then keep searching!

THE DECLARATION OF INDEPENDENCE

Thomas Jefferson's Declaration of Independence was presented to the Continental Congress on June 28, 1776. On July 2, 12 of 13 colonial delegates voted in support of Richard Henry Lee's resolution for independence. Fight for your right to find the New York delegate who didn't vote.

WORLD'S COLUMBIAN EXPOSITION

Feast your eyes on these strange sights in the Agriculture Building: a 1,500-pound chocolate Venus de Milo statue, a Liberty Bell made of oranges, and a 22,000-pound hunk of cheese from Canada. Can you also pick out the U.S. map made entirely of pickles? Now find five more pickles at the fair.

Next door to the Electricity Building was the Mines & Mining Building. Here you'll find a solid silver statue. Can you also spy a model of the Statue of Liberty made entirely of salt?

THE 1960s

Did you know *Barbie* dolls were introduced in 1959? The dolls were an instant hit, making them one of the most popular toys of the 1960s. To get boys in on the action, another toy manufacturer came up with *G.I. Joe* action figures, the first toys of this sort for boys. Hunt down a *G.I. Joe*.

In 1969, the first human walked on the moon. Neil Armstrong opened the hatch on the *Eagle* and went down the ladder to the moon's surface. Buzz Aldrin then joined Armstrong, and for 51 minutes the two astronauts set up scientific experiments and collected lunar samples. Aldrin planted an American flag on the moon. Flag down four U.S. flags.

THE CIVIL WAR

Before the war, the South bought its cloth from mills in the North. President Lincoln ordered a blockade of Southern ports so no ships could deliver fabric for clothing. Hoop skirts used too much fabric, so Southern ladies had to wear smaller straight skirts. Hop to it and find this hoop skirt.

Thousands of boys from the North and the South took part in the war. Recruiters weren't supposed to accept anyone younger than 18, but some as young as 11 signed up as drummer boys. Play around and find a drummer boy.

To provide a proper burial for Union soldiers, people raised money for a national cemetery in Gettysburg. The cemetery was dedicated on November 19, 1863, with a speech by President Lincoln known as the Gettysburg Address. He spoke of the importance of honoring the dead by reuniting the country. Look out for Lincoln in Gettysburg.

U.S. PRESIDENTS

Lyndon Baines Johnson (1963–1969) declared war on poverty in the United States. His programs included a Job Corps for disadvantaged teenagers and Head Start for preschool children. He pushed through the Voting Rights Act, which made it possible for African-Americans to register to vote. Sniff out Johnson's pet beagles, Him and Her.

HARRY S. TRUMAN After Franklin D. Roosevelt's death, Vice President Harry S. Truman (1945–1953) became the nation's leader. He made the very tough decision to drop an atomic bomb on Japan in August 1945 to end World War II. The *S* in Truman's name is not an abbreviation of his middle name—it stands for nothing! Truman's nameplate has "s"-caped from his desk. Can you find it?